Longman Structural Readers: Background
Stage 2

Customs and Traditions in Britain

Stephen Rabley

GW00370467

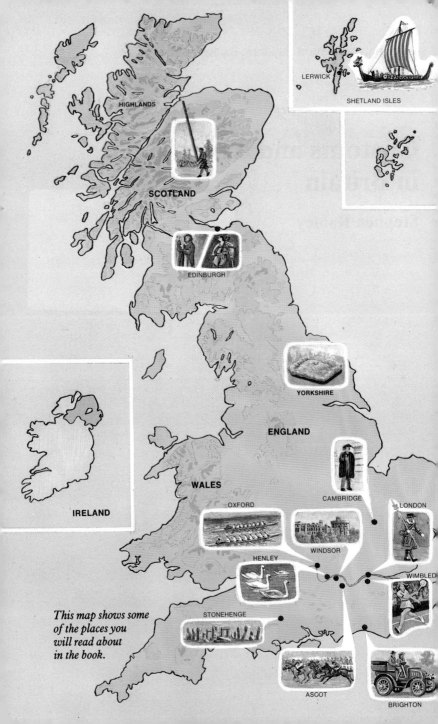

LERWICK

SHETLAND ISLES

HIGHLANDS

SCOTLAND

EDINBURGH

YORKSHIRE

ENGLAND

WALES

CAMBRIDGE

LONDON

IRELAND

OXFORD

WINDSOR

WIMBLEDON

HENLEY

STONEHENGE

This map shows some of the places you will read about in the book.

ASCOT

BRIGHTON

Introduction

Some British customs and traditions are famous all over the world. Bowler hats, tea and talking about the weather, for example. But what about the others? Who was Guy Fawkes? Why does the Queen have two birthdays? And what is the word "pub" short for? You can find the answers here in this book on traditional British life.

From Scotland to Cornwall, Britain is full of customs and traditions. A lot of them have very long histories. Some are funny and some are strange. But they're all interesting. There are all the traditions of British sport and music. There's the long menu of traditional British food. There are many royal occasions. There are songs, sayings and superstitions. They are all part of the British way of life.

London, Britain's capital city, is full of traditions.

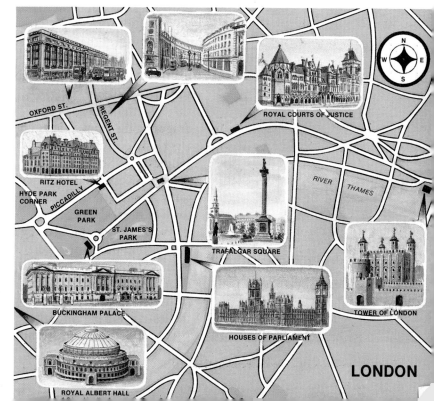

LONDON

A year in Britain

JANUARY
Up-Helly-Aa

The Shetlands are islands near Scotland. In the ninth century, men from Norway came to the Shetlands. These were the Vikings. They came to Britain in ships and carried away animals, gold, and sometimes women and children, too.

Now, 1,000 years later, people in the Shetlands remember the Vikings with a festival. They call the festival "Up-Helly-Aa".

Every winter the people of Lerwick, a town in the Shetlands, make a model of a ship. It's a Viking "long-ship", with the head of a dragon at the front. Then, on Up-Helly-Aa night in January, the Shetlanders dress in Viking clothes. They carry the ship through the town to the sea. There they burn it. They do this because the Vikings put their dead men in ships and burned them. But there aren't any men in the modern ships. Now the festival is a party for the people of the Shetland Islands.

FEBRUARY
St Valentine's Day

St Valentine is the saint of people in love, and St Valentine's Day is February 14th. On that day, people send Valentine cards and presents to their husbands, wives, boyfriends and girlfriends. You can also send a card to a person you don't know. But traditionally you must never write your name on it. Some British newspapers have a page for Valentine's Day messages on February 14th.

MARCH
St David's Day

March 1st is a very important day for Welsh people. It's St David's Day. He's the "patron" or national saint of Wales. On March 1st, the Welsh celebrate St David's Day and wear daffodils in the buttonholes of their coats or jackets.

APRIL
April Fool's Day

April 1st is April Fool's Day in Britain. This is a very old tradition from the Middle Ages (between the fifth and fifteenth centuries). At that time the servants were masters for one day of the year. They gave orders to their masters, and their masters had to obey.

Now April Fool's Day is different. It's a day for jokes and tricks.

MAY
May Day

May 1st was an important day in the Middle Ages. In the very early morning, young girls went to the fields and washed their faces with dew. They believed this made them very beautiful for a year after that. Also on May Day the young men of each village tried to win prizes with their bows and arrows, and people danced round the maypole.

Many English villages still have a maypole, and on May 1st, the villagers dance round it. You can see one in the picture below.

JUNE
Midsummer's Day

Midsummer's Day, June 24th, is the longest day of the year.
On that day you can see a very old custom at Stonehenge,
in Wiltshire, England. Stonehenge is one of Europe's biggest
stone circles. A lot of the stones are ten or twelve metres high.
It's also very old. The earliest part of Stonehenge is nearly
5,000 years old.

But what was Stonehenge? A holy place? A market? Or was
it a kind of calendar? We think the Druids used it for a
calendar. The Druids were the priests in Britain 2,000 years
ago. They used the sun and the stones at Stonehenge to know
the start of months and seasons. There are Druids in Britain
today, too. And every June 24th a lot of them go to
Stonehenge. On that morning the sun shines on one famous
stone — the Heel stone. For the Druids this is a very
important moment in the year. But for a lot of British people
it's just a strange old custom.

7

OCTOBER
Hallowe'en

October 31st is Hallowe'en, and you can expect to meet witches and ghosts that night. Hallowe'en is an old word for "Hallows Evening", the night before "All Hallows" or "All Saints' Day".

On that one night of the year, ghosts and witches are free. Well, that's the traditional story. A long time ago people were afraid and stayed at home on Hallowe'en. But now in Britain it's a time for fun. There are always a lot of parties on October 31st. At these parties people wear masks and they dress as ghosts and witches, or as Dracula or Frankenstein's monster. And some people make special Hallowe'en lamps from a large fruit — the pumpkin.

First they take out the middle of the pumpkin. Then they cut holes for the eyes, nose and mouth. Finally they put a candle inside the pumpkin.

NOVEMBER
Guy Fawkes' Day

November 5th is Guy Fawkes' Day in Britain. All over the country people build wood fires, or "bonfires", in their gardens. On top of each bonfire is a guy. That's a figure of Guy Fawkes. People make guys with straw, old clothes and newspapers. But before November 5th, children use their guys to make money. They stand in the street and shout

"Penny for the guy". Then they spend the money on fireworks. But how did this tradition start? Who was Guy Fawkes and why do the British remember him on November 5th?

On November 5th 1605, Guy Fawkes tried to kill King James I. He and a group of friends put a bomb under the Houses of Parliament in London. But the King's men found the bomb — and they found Guy Fawkes, too. They took him to the Tower of London and there the King's men cut off his head.

DECEMBER
Christmas and the New Year

There are lots of Christmas and New Year traditions in Britain. For example . . .

London's Christmas decorations

Every year the people of Norway give the city of London a present. It's a big Christmas tree and it stands in Trafalgar Square. Also in central London, Oxford Street and Regent Street always have beautiful decorations at Christmas. Thousands of people come to look at them.

Cards, trees and mistletoe

In 1846 the first Christmas cards began in Britain. That was five years after the first Christmas tree. Queen Victoria's husband, Prince Albert, brought this German tradition (he was German) to Britain. He and the Queen had a Christmas tree at Windsor Castle in 1841. A few years after, nearly every house in Britain had one.

Traditionally people decorate their trees on Christmas Eve — that's December 24th. They take down the decorations twelve

days later, on Twelfth Night (January 5th).

An older tradition is Christmas mistletoe. People put a piece of this green plant with its white berries over a door. Mistletoe brings good luck, people say. Also, at Christmas British people kiss their friends and family under the mistletoe.

good king
Wenceslas

Traditional

Arranged by Norman Lloyd

1. Good King Wen - ces - las look'd out, On the feast of Ste - phen,
2. "Hith - er, page, and stand by me, If thou knows't it tell - ing,
3. "Bring me flesh, and bring me wine, Bring me pine - logs hith - er:
4. "Sire, the night is dark - er now, And the wind grows strong - er;
5. In his mas - ter's steps he trod, Where the snow lay dint - ed;

When the snow lay round - a - bout, Deep and crisp and e - ven.
Yon - der peas - ant, who is he? Where and what his dwell - ing?"
Thou and I shall see him dine, When we bear them thith - er."
Fails my heart I know not how; I can go no long - er."
Heat was in the ver - y sod Which the Saint had print - ed.

Bright - ly shone the moon that night, Though the frost was cru - el,
"Sire, he lives a good league hence, Un - der - neath the moun - tain,
Page and mon - arch, forth they went, Forth they went to - geth - er;
"Mark my foot - steps, my good page, Tread thou in them bold - ly;
There - fore, Chris - tian men, be sure, Wealth or rank pos - sess - ing,

When a poor man came in sight, Gath - 'ring win - ter fu - el,
Right a - gainst the for - est fence, By Saint Ag - nes' foun - tain."
Through the rude wind's wild la - ment And the bit - ter weath - er.
Thou shalt find the win - ter's rage Freeze thy blood less cold - ly."
Ye who now will bless the poor, Shall your - selves find bless - ing.

12

Carols

Before Christmas, groups of singers go from house to house. They collect money and sing traditional Christmas songs or carols. There are a lot of very popular British Christmas carols. Three famous ones are: "Good King Wenceslas", "The Holly and The Ivy" and "We Three Kings".

Christmas Eve

British children don't open their presents on December 24th. Father Christmas brings their presents in the night. Then they open them on the morning of the 25th.

There's another name for Father Christmas in Britain — Santa Claus. That comes from the European name for him — Saint Nicholas. In the traditional story he lives at the North Pole. But now he lives in big shops in towns and cities all over Britain. Well, that's where children see him in November and December. Then on Christmas Eve he visits every house. He climbs down the chimney and leaves lots of presents. Some people leave something for *him*, too. A glass of wine and some biscuits, for example.

Christmas Day

In Britain the most important meal on December 25th is Christmas dinner. Nearly all Christmas food is traditional, but a lot of the traditions are not very old. For example, there were no turkeys in Britain before 1800. And even in the nineteenth century, goose was the traditional meat at Christmas. But not now.

A twentieth-century British Christmas dinner is roast turkey with carrots, potatoes, peas, Brussels sprouts and gravy. There are sausages and bacon too. Then, after the turkey, there's Christmas pudding. You can read about that in the chapter on food.

Crackers are also usual at Christmas dinner. These came to Britain from China in the nineteenth century. Two people pull a cracker. Usually there's a small toy in the middle. Often there's a joke on a piece of paper, too. Most of the jokes in Christmas crackers are not very good. Here's an example:

CUSTOMER: Waiter, there's a frog in my soup.
WAITER: Yes, sir, the fly's on holiday.

Boxing Day

December 26th is Boxing Day. Traditionally boys from the shops in each town asked for money at Christmas. They went from house to house on December 26th and took boxes made of wood with them. At each house people gave them money. This was a Christmas present. So the name of December 26th doesn't come from the sport of boxing — it comes from the boys' wooden boxes. Now, Boxing Day is an extra holiday after Christmas Day.

First Footing

In Scotland the name for New Year's Eve is Hogmanay. After midnight people visit their friends. And they take a present — a piece of coal. Why? Because traditionally the first visitor of the year must carry coal into the house. This is "first footing". It brings good luck. It also helps to make a fire in the middle of winter.

New Year Resolutions

What are your worst faults? Do you want to change them? In Britain a lot of people make New Year Resolutions on the evening of December 31st. For example, "I'll get up early every morning next year", or "I'll clean my shoes every day." But there's a problem. Most people forget their New Year Resolutions on January 2nd.

Royal traditions

THE TROOPING OF THE COLOUR

The Queen is the only person in Britain with two birthdays. Her real birthday is on April 21st, but she has an "official" birthday, too. That's on the second Saturday in June. And on the Queen's official birthday, there is a traditional ceremony called the Trooping of the Colour. It's a big parade with brass bands and hundreds of soldiers at Horse Guards' Parade in London. A "regiment" of the Queen's soldiers, the Guards, march in front of her. At the front of the parade is the regiment's flag or "colour".

The Guards are trooping the colour. Thousands of Londoners and visitors watch in Horse Guards' Parade. And millions of people at home watch it on television.

THE CHANGING OF THE GUARD

This happens every day at Buckingham Palace, the Queen's home in London. Soldiers stand in front of the palace. Each morning these soldiers (the "guard") change. One group leaves and another arrives. In summer and winter tourists stand outside the palace at 11.30 every morning and watch the Changing of the Guard.

MAUNDY MONEY

Maundy Thursday is the day before Good Friday, at Easter. On that day the Queen gives Maundy money to a group of old people. This tradition is over 1,000 years old. At one time the king or queen washed the feet of poor, old people on Maundy Thursday. That stopped in 1754.

SWAN UPPING

Here's a very different royal tradition. On the River Thames there are hundreds of swans. A lot of these beautiful white birds belong, traditionally, to the king or queen. In July the young swans on the Thames are about two months old. Then the Queen's swan keeper goes, in a boat, from London Bridge to Henley. He looks at all the young swans and marks the royal ones. The name of this strange but interesting custom is Swan Upping.

THE QUEEN'S TELEGRAM

This custom is not very old, but it's for very old people. On his or her one hundredth birthday, a British person gets a telegram from the Queen.

THE BIRTHDAY HONOURS LIST AND THE NEW YEAR'S HONOURS LIST

Twice a year at Buckingham Palace, the Queen gives titles or "honours", once in January and once in June.

There are a lot of different honours. Here are a few:

C.B.E. — Companion of the British Empire
O.B.E. — Order of the British Empire
M.B.E. — Member of the British Empire
(These honours began in the nineteenth century. Then Britain had an empire.)

Knighthood — a knight has "Sir" before his name. A new knight kneels in front of the Queen. She touches first his right shoulder, then his left shoulder with a sword. Then she says "Arise, Sir . . . [his first name]", and the knight stands.

Peerage — a peer is a lord. Peers sit in the House of Lords. That's one part of the Houses of Parliament. The other part is the House of Commons. Peers call the House of Commons "another place".

Dame/Baroness — these are two of the highest honours for a woman.

THE STATE OPENING OF PARLIAMENT

Parliament, not the Royal Family, controls modern Britain. But traditionally the Queen opens Parliament every autumn. She travels from Buckingham Palace to the Houses of Parliament in a gold carriage — the Irish State Coach. At the Houses of Parliament the Queen sits on a "throne" in the House of Lords. Then she reads the "Queen's Speech". At the State Opening of Parliament the Queen wears a crown. She wears other jewels from the Crown Jewels, too.

THE ORDER OF THE GARTER CEREMONY

The Order of the Garter ceremony has a long history. King Edward III started the Order in the fourteenth century. At that time, the people in the Order were the twenty-four bravest knights in England. Now the knights of the Order aren't all soldiers. They're members of the House of Lords, church leaders or politicians. There are some foreign knights, too. For example, the King of Norway, the Grand Duke of Luxembourg and the Emperor of Japan. They're called Extra Knights of the Garter. The Queen is the Sovereign of the

The ceremony of the Garter

Order of the Garter. But she isn't the only royal person in the Order. Prince Charles and Prince Philip are Royal Knights, and the Queen Mother is a Lady of the Garter.

In June the Order has a traditional ceremony at Windsor Castle. This is the Queen's favourite castle. It's also the home of the Order of the Garter. All the knights walk from the castle to St George's Chapel, the royal church at Windsor. They wear the traditional clothes or "robes" of the Order. These robes are very heavy. In fact King Edward VIII once called them "ridiculous". But they're an important part of one of Britain's oldest traditions.

THE QUEEN'S CHRISTMAS SPEECH

Now here's a modern royal custom. On Christmas Day at 3.00 in the afternoon, the Queen makes a speech on radio and TV. It's ten minutes long. In it she talks to the people of the United Kingdom and the Commonwealth. The Commonwealth is a large group of countries. In the past they were all in the British Empire. Australia, India, Canada and New Zealand are among the 49 members.

The B.B.C. (the British Broadcasting Corporation) sends the Queen's speech to every Commonwealth country. In her speech the Queen talks about the past year. Traditionally in speeches, kings or queens say "we", not "I". Queen Elizabeth II doesn't do this. She says "My husband and I", or just "I".

The Queen doesn't make her speech on Christmas Day. She films it a few weeks before. Then she spends Christmas with her family at Windsor. Does she watch the speech on TV? Nobody knows.

Songs, sayings and superstitions

There are thousands of traditional songs and sayings in English. Many of them tell stories about British history. For example, here's one about the Great Plague.

Ring-a-ring-a roses
A pocket full of posies
A-tishoo, a-tishoo
We all fall down.

The Great Plague was an illness and it killed millions of people in Europe in the seventeenth century. One of the signs of the illness was a circle of red marks. They looked like roses, and that explains the first line of the song. In the second line, "posies" are small bunches of flowers. People carried flowers because of the smell of the Plague. "A-tishoo" is the sound of a sneeze. That was another sign of the Plague. Then, after a few days, people "fell down" or died.

21

How many of these traditional songs do you know?

Happy Birthday To You — You sing this song at birthday parties. People all over the world sing it.

Auld Lang Syne — This is a song from Scotland. Most people only sing it once a year, on New Year's Eve. "Auld Lang Syne" means "a long time ago". The song says, "we must never forget old friends".

God Save The Queen — This is Britain's national song or "anthem."

GOD SAVE THE QUEEN

God save our gracious Queen,
Long live our noble Queen,
   God save the Queen —
Send her victorious,
Happy and glorious,
Long to reign over us,
   God save the Queen.

For He's A Jolly Good Fellow — This song says, "we all like this person". It can, of course, be "For *she's* a jolly good fellow", too.

Greensleeves — This is a sixteenth-century English song. Some people think that King Henry VIII wrote it.

22

FOR HE'S A JOLLY GOOD FELLOW

For he's a jolly good fellow,
For he's a jolly good fellow,
For he's a jolly good fellow,
And so say all of us! —

GREENSLEEVES

English Folk-tune

Alas, my love, you do me wrong
To cast me off discourteously,
And I have lovéd you so long,
Delighting in your company.
Chorus: Greensleeves was all my joy,
Greensleeves was my delight;
Greensleeves was my heart of gold,
And who but my lady Greensleeves?

SUPERSTITIONS

Do you believe in good luck and bad luck? Most people in the world have some superstitions. These are a few British superstitions with long traditions.

Good Luck

- Black cats are lucky.

- Clover is a small plant. Usually it has three leaves, but a few have four. A clover with four leaves brings good luck.

- A horseshoe over the door of a new home brings good luck. But the horseshoe must be the right way up. The luck runs out of a horseshoe if it's upside down.

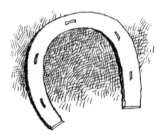

- On the first day of the month it's lucky to say "White rabbits".
- It's good luck to see two magpies (large black and white birds).
- Catch falling leaves in autumn and you'll have good luck. Every leaf means a lucky month in the next year.

Bad Luck

- Never open an umbrella in the house. That's very bad luck.
- Never break a mirror — that means seven years' bad luck.
- It's bad luck to see just one magpie.

- Don't walk under a ladder.
- Don't walk past somebody on the stairs.
- The number thirteen is very unlucky (and Friday the 13th is a very unlucky date).

SAYINGS

Here are ten British "proverbs" or sayings.

1 *Nothing ventured nothing gained.*
You have to try or you won't get anything.

2 *One man's meat is another man's poison.*
People often don't like the same things.

3 *The other man's grass is always greener.*
You always think that other people's lives are better than yours.

4 *Don't look a gift horse in the mouth.*
Don't question good luck.

5 *Every cloud has a silver lining.*
There's always something good in bad times.

6 *It's no use crying over spilt milk.*
Don't be too sad after a small accident.

7 *Out of the frying pan, into the fire.*
From one problem to another.

8 *Fools rush in where angels fear to tread.*
Stupid people do things that other people never do.

9 *You can lead a horse to water but you cannot make it drink.*
You can give a person a chance, but you can't make him or her take it.

10 *A stitch in time saves nine.*
Act early and you can save a lot of trouble.

Food and drink

THE ENGLISH BREAKFAST

In a real English breakfast you have fried eggs, bacon, sausage, tomato and mushrooms. Then there's toast and marmalade. There's an interesting story about the word "marmalade". It may come from the French "Marie est malade", or "Mary is ill." That's because a seventeenth-century Queen of Scotland, Mary Queen of Scots, liked it. She always asked for French orange jam when she was ill.

PANCAKES

British people eat pancakes on Shrove Tuesday in February or March. For pancakes you need flour, eggs and milk. Then you eat them with sugar and lemon. In some parts of Britain there are pancake races on Shrove Tuesday. People race with a frying pan in one hand. They have to "toss" the pancake, throw it in the air and catch it again in the frying pan.

ROAST BEEF AND YORKSHIRE PUDDING

This is the traditional Sunday lunch from Yorkshire in the north of England. It is now popular all over Britain. Yorkshire pudding is not sweet. It's a simple mixture of eggs, flour and milk, but it's delicious.

Two common vegetables with roast beef and Yorkshire pudding are Brussels sprouts and carrots. And of course there's always gravy. That's a thick, brown sauce. You make gravy with the juice from the meat.

HAGGIS

Haggis is a traditional food from Scotland. You make it with meat, onions, flour, salt and pepper. Then you boil it in the skin from a sheep's stomach — yes, a sheep's stomach.

In Scotland, people eat haggis on Burns Night. Robert Burns (Scots people call him "Rabbie" Burns), was a Scottish poet in the eighteenth century. Every year Scots people all over the world remember him and read his poems.

TEA

Tea is Britain's favourite drink. It's also a meal in the afternoon. You can eat tea at home or in a hotel. Tea at the Ritz hotel in London is very good. You can drink Indian or China tea. There are cucumber sandwiches and scones. (Scones are plain cakes. You eat them with jam and cream.) There are chocolate cakes and cream cakes too.

CHRISTMAS PUDDING

Some people make this pudding months before Christmas. A lot of families have their own Christmas pudding recipes. Some, for example, use a lot of brandy. Others put in a lot of fruit or add a silver coin for good luck.

Real Christmas puddings always have a piece of holly on the top. Holly bushes and trees have red berries at Christmastime, and so people use holly to decorate their houses for Christmas. The holly on the pudding is part of the decoration. Also, you can pour brandy over the pudding and light it with a match.

HOT CROSS BUNS

The first Christians in Rome made hot cross buns two thousand years ago. But now they're an Easter tradition in Britain. Here's a story about hot cross buns. In 1800 a widow lived in a house in East London. Her only son was a sailor and went to sea. Every year she made hot cross buns and kept one for him. He never came back, but she kept a bun for him every year. Then, after many years, she died. Now, her house is a pub. It's called "The Widow's Son". For a long time people remembered the widow. Every Easter they put a hot cross bun in a special basket in the pub. Now the tradition is different. The owner of the pub sells the special hot cross bun. Then he gives the money to the British Sailors' Society.

PUBS

Pubs are an important part of British life. People talk, eat, drink, meet their friends and relax there. They are open at lunchtime and again in the evening. But they close at 11.00 (10.30 on Sundays). This surprises a lot of tourists. But you can always go to Scotland — the pubs close later there!

The word "pub" is short for "public house". There are thousands in Britain, and they nearly all sell pub lunches. One

of these is a Ploughman's Lunch, a very simple meal. It's just bread and cheese.

Pubs also sell beer. (British beer is always warm.) The traditional kind is called "real ale". That's a very strong beer from an old recipe.

An important custom in pubs is "buying a round". In a group, one person buys all the others a drink. This is a "round". Then one by one all the other people buy rounds, too.

If they are with friends, British people sometimes lift their glasses before they drink and say "Cheers". This means "Good luck".

In the pubs in south-west England there's another traditional drink — scrumpy. You make scrumpy with apples, but it's not a simple fruit juice. It's very, very strong.

Pub names often have a long tradition. Some come from the thirteenth or fourteenth century.

Every pub has a name and every pub has a sign above its door. The sign shows a picture of the pub's name.

Here are a few common pub names in Britain

Flags and emblems

The United Kingdom's flag is the Union Jack. It's red, white and blue.

Here are the flags of England, Scotland, Northern Ireland and Wales, and the Union Jack.

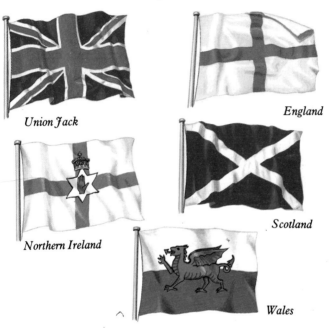

Union Jack

England

Northern Ireland

Scotland

Wales

Each country also has a national "emblem" or sign. The English emblem is a red rose. The Welsh emblem is a vegetable or flower — a leek or a daffodil. The Scottish emblem is a wild plant — a thistle. And the Irish emblem is another wild plant — a shamrock.

It's traditional in Britain to wear your country's emblem on its saint's day. The leek doesn't go in a buttonhole, so the Welsh often wear a daffodil. These are Britain's patron saints and their days.

England — St George — April 23rd.
Ireland — St Patrick — March 17th.
Scotland — St Andrew — November 30th.
Wales — St David — March 1st.

The Scots, Welsh and English don't really celebrate their national saint's days. But St Patrick's Day is important for Irish people all over the world. In New York, for example, the Irish people always have a big St Patrick's Day parade.

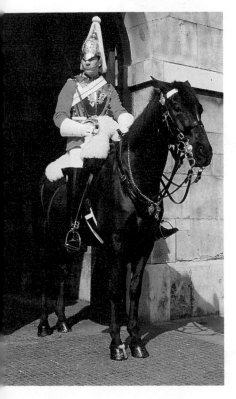

A Horse Guard

Costumes and clothes

Many British costumes and uniforms have a long history. One is the uniform of the Beefeaters at the Tower of London. (See the picture on page 45.) This came first from France. Another is the uniform of the Horse Guards at Horse Guards' Parade, not far from Buckingham Palace. Thousands of visitors take photographs of the Horse Guards, but the Guards never move or smile. In fact some visitors think the Guards aren't real. And that brings us to...

. . . Britannia. She wears traditional clothes, too. But she's not a real person. She is a symbol of Britain.

Lots of ordinary clothes have a long tradition. The famous bowler hat, for example. A man called Beaulieu ('bju:li) made the first one in 1850.

The very cold winters in the Crimea in the war of 1853—56 gave us the names of the cardigan and the balaclava. Lord Cardigan led the Light Brigade at the Battle of Balaclava (1854). A "cardigan" is now a warm woollen short coat with buttons, and a "balaclava" is a woollen hat.

Another British soldier, Wellington, gave his name to a pair of boots. They have a shorter name today — "Wellies".

Sport

THE UNIVERSITY BOAT RACE

Oxford and Cambridge are Britain's two oldest universities. In the nineteenth century, rowing was a popular sport at both of them. In 1829 the universities agreed to have a race. They raced on the river Thames and the Oxford boat won. That started a tradition. Now, every Spring, the University Boat Race goes from Putney to Mortlake on the Thames. That's 6.7 kilometres. The Cambridge rowers wear light blue shirts and the Oxford rowers wear dark blue. There are eight men in each boat. There's also a "cox". The cox controls the boat. Traditionally coxes are men, but Susan Brown became the first woman cox in 1981. She was the cox for Oxford and they won.

ROYAL ASCOT

Ascot is a small, quiet town in the south of England. But in June for one week it becomes the centre of the horse-racing world. It's called Royal Ascot because the Queen always goes to Ascot. She has a lot of racehorses and likes to watch racing. But Ascot week isn't just for horseracing. It's for fashion, too. One woman, Mrs Gertrude Shilling, always wears very big hats. You can see the racecourse in the picture below.

WIMBLEDON

The world's most famous tennis tournament is Wimbledon. It started at a small club in south London in the nineteenth century. Now a lot of the nineteenth-century traditions have changed. For example, the women players don't have to wear long skirts. And the men players don't have to wear long trousers.

Traditions change — a tennis match at Wimbledon in 1911

But other traditions haven't changed at Wimbledon. The courts are still grass, and visitors still eat strawberries and cream. The language of tennis hasn't changed either. Did you know that "love" (zero) comes from "l'oeuf" (the egg) in French?

THE LONDON TO BRIGHTON VINTAGE CAR RALLY

"Vintage" cars have to be more than fifty years old and in very good condition. Lots of people keep or collect vintage cars. And on the first Sunday in November there's a race or "rally" for them. It starts in London and it finishes in Brighton, a town on the south coast of England. That's a distance of seventy kilometres.

Before 1896 a man with a red flag had to walk in front

of cars. In 1896 that changed. A group of happy drivers broke their flags and drove to Brighton. There they had a party. Now the rally is a sporting tradition.

A lot of the people in the rally wear "vintage" clothes, too. In a 1910 car, for example, the driver and passengers wear 1910 hats and coats.

BOXING DAY HUNTS

Traditionally Boxing Day is a day for foxhunting. The huntsmen and huntswomen ride horses. They use dogs, too. The dogs (fox hounds) follow the smell of the fox. Then the huntsmen and huntswomen follow the hounds.

Before a Boxing Day hunt, the huntsmen and huntswomen drink hot wine. But the tradition of the December 26th hunt is changing. Now, some people want to stop Boxing Day hunts (and other hunts, too). They don't like foxhunting. For them it's not a sport — it's cruel.

THE HIGHLAND GAMES

This sporting tradition is Scottish. In the Highlands (the mountains of Scotland) families, or "clans", started the Games hundreds of years ago.

Some of the sports at the Games are international: the high jump and the long jump, for example. But other sports happen only at the Highland Games. One is tossing the caber. "Tossing" means throwing, and a "caber" is a long, heavy piece of wood. In tossing the caber you lift the caber (it can be five or six metres tall). Then you throw it in front of you.

At the Highland Games a lot of men wear kilts. These are traditional Scottish skirts for men. But they're not all the same. Each clan has a different "tartan". That's the name for the pattern on the kilt. So at the Highland Games there are traditional sports and traditional clothes. And there's traditional music, too, from Scotland's national instrument — the bagpipes. The bagpipes are very loud. They say Scots soldiers played them before a battle. The noise frightened the soldiers on the other side.

THE GLORIOUS TWELFTH

The grouse is a small bird. It lives in the north of England and in Scotland. It tastes very good. But people can't shoot grouse all the time. They can only shoot them for a few months of the year. And the first day of the grouse "season" is August 12th. On that day, "the glorious twelfth", hunters send their grouse to London restaurants. There, people wait for the first grouse of the year. But there's good news for the grouse, too — the season ends on December 10th each year!

Grouse shooting ▶

▲ *Tossing the caber*

▲ *Pipes and drums*

The Arts

THE PROMS

Do you like classical music? Every summer in London there are two months of special concerts at the Royal Albert Hall. These are the "Proms". Sir Henry Wood started the Proms (short for "promenade" concerts) in the nineteenth century. Now they're a tradition in British musical life.

A lot of young people go to the Proms. They buy cheap tickets and stand up for the concerts. They are the "promenaders". There are seats too, but the tickets for those cost more.

The music at the Proms comes from some of the best singers and orchestras in the world. And on the last night there's a big party at the Royal Albert Hall. People bring balloons and paper hats. The orchestra plays popular classical music and at the end everyone sings "Rule Britannia".

THEATRE TRADITIONS

Actors have lots of traditions and superstitions. For example, you don't say "good luck" to an actor. You say "break a leg". It's strange but true. "Good luck" is bad luck. Also, actors never say the name of Shakespeare's famous play "Macbeth". They always call it "The Scottish Play". In theatres the name Macbeth brings bad luck.

A third tradition is about whistling. You must never whistle in a theatre dressing room. Someone who whistles must go out of the room and turn around three times. Only after that, can they knock on the door and come in again.

THE EDINBURGH FESTIVAL

Every August, Edinburgh in Scotland has the biggest art festival in Europe. There are plays, concerts and exhibitions from countries all over the world. That's the "official" festival. But there's an "unofficial" festival, too. This is called the Edinburgh "Fringe". At the Fringe, visitors can see cheaper concerts and plays by students.

PANTOMIME

Pantomimes are traditional British plays. They are for children, and you see them at Christmas. Some famous pantomimes are: *Cinderella, Aladdin, Peter Pan* and *Babes in the Wood*. A lot of these stories are very old. In pantomime there's always a young hero. He's the Principal Boy, but the actor is usually a woman. Also, there's always a funny, old woman. She's the Pantomime

Cinderella

Dame, but the actor is always a man.

41

EISTEDDFODS

An Eisteddfod is an arts festival in Wales. People sing and read their poetry in the Welsh language. The Welsh name for these poets is "bards". People also play music. The harp is very popular in Wales. You can always hear harp music at an Eisteddfod. But Eisteddfods aren't just festivals. They're also competitions to find the best singers, musicians and poets in Wales.

A Welsh bard

London

Britain's capital city is full of traditions and customs. Here's a guide to just a few of them. (There is a map of London on page 3.)

THE LORD MAYOR'S SHOW

Every year there's a new Lord Mayor of London. The Mayor is the city's traditional leader. And the second Saturday in November is always the day for the Lord Mayor's Show. This ceremony is over six hundred years old. It's also London's biggest parade.

The Lord Mayor drives to the Royal Courts of Justice

(near Fleet Street) in a coach. The coach is two hundred years old. It's red and gold and it has six horses. You can see it in the picture above.

There's also a big parade. People make special costumes and act stories from London's history.

THE NOTTING HILL CARNIVAL

This is Europe's biggest street carnival. A lot of people in the Notting Hill area of London come from the West Indies — a group of islands in the Caribbean. And for two days in August, Notting Hill *is* the West Indies. There's West Indian food and music in the streets. There's also a big parade and people dance day and night.

PEARLY KINGS AND QUEENS

Londoners from the east of the city are "Cockneys". There are a lot of traditional Cockney expressions. For example, Cockneys don't say "stairs" — they say "apples and pears". And they don't say "face" — they say "boat race". This is Cockney rhyming slang.

The Cockneys have kings and queens, too — the "pearly" kings and queens. They wear special costumes on important days. Each costume has thousands of pearl buttons.

THE TOWER OF LONDON

William the Conqueror and his army landed in England from France in the year 1066. In 1078 he started to build the Tower of London. Now, nine hundred years later, this famous castle is full of history and tradition.

The guards at the Tower are called Beefeaters. Their name comes from a French word — *boufitiers*. Boufitiers were guards in the palaces of French kings. They protected the king's food.

You will see some large, black birds at the Tower of London. These are the ravens at the Tower. Ravens have lived at the Tower of London for hundreds of years.

People go to see the Beefeaters and the ravens, but that's not all. Visitors to the Tower go to see the Crown Jewels, too. There are eight crowns. There are also a lot of other very famous jewels in the jewel room. In fact the Crown Jewels are the biggest tourist attraction in London.

In the evening there is another old custom at the Tower of London — the Ceremony of the Keys. At 9.53 exactly, the Beefeaters close the Tower. Then at 10.00 they give the keys to the Governor of the Tower. That's because a long time ago the Tower of London was a prison for important prisoners: Anne Boleyn (Henry VIII's second wife), Sir Walter Raleigh, Guy Fawkes, and many others.

A Beefeater

The Crown Jewels

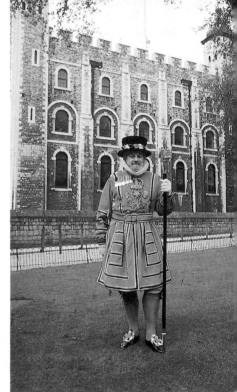

Everyday life

TALKING ABOUT THE WEATHER

The British talk about the weather a lot. For example, "Isn't it a beautiful morning?" or, "Very cold today, isn't it?" They talk about the weather because it changes so often. Wind, rain, sun, cloud, snow — they can all happen in a British winter — or a British summer.

QUEUEING

At British banks, shops, cinemas, theatres or bus stops you can always see people in queues. They stand in a line and wait quietly, often for a long time. Each new person stands at the end of the queue — sometimes in rain, wind or snow.

SHAKING HANDS

Hundreds of years ago, soldiers began this custom. They shook hands to show that they didn't have a sword. Now, shaking hands is a custom in most countries. In Britain you don't shake hands with your friends and family. But you *do* shake hands when you meet a person for the first time. You also say "How do you do?" This is not really a question, it's a tradition. The correct answer is exactly the same, "How do you do?"

CARDS

The British send birthday cards and often give birthday presents. There are cards for other days, too:
Christmas cards, Valentine's Day cards, Mother's Day cards, Father's Day cards, Easter cards, Wedding Anniversary cards, Good Luck cards, "Congratulations On Your New Baby" cards, and "Get Well Soon" cards.

PARTIES

It's the custom to have a party to celebrate . . .
A person's birthday
A new house
Christmas (at home, and often in offices, too)
An engagement (a promise to marry)
A wedding (marriage)
New Year's Eve

Pearson Education Limited,
Edinburgh Gate, Harlow,
Essex CM20 2JE, England

© Longman Group UK Limited 1986

First published 1986
Fourteenth impression 1999

Set in 11/13pt Plantin Linotron 202

Printed in China
GCC/14

ISBN 0-582-74908-5

Acknowledgements

We are grateful to the following for permission to reproduce copyright photographs:
Ace Photo Agency for page 32; Aspect Picture Library Limited for pages 17 (top)/Bob
Davis and 39 (top left); BBC Hulton Picture Library for pages 21 and 36 (top); British
Tourist Authority for pages 10 (bottom left), 15, 35 (bottom), 41 and 42; J. Allan
Cash Photo Library for pages 6, 8 (left), 11 (top); 30 (top left, middle left, middle
right), 43 (bottom) and 44; Colorsport for page 35 (top); Daily Telegraph Colour
Library for page 7; Susan Griggs Agency/Adam Woolfitt for page 4 (top and bottom)
and 13; Longman Photo Unit for page 5; Mary Evans Picture Library for page 33;
The Photo Source Limited for pages 19 and 40; The Photographers Library for page
27 (bottom); Pictor International Limited for pages 8 (right) and 39 (top right);
Picturepoint Limited for pages 9, 10 (top), 14, 27 (top), 29, 30 (bottom left and right),
39 (bottom), 43 (top) and 45 (left); The Press Association Limited for page 17
(bottom); Rex Features Limited for page 10 (bottom right), 20 and 36 (bottom); Tony
Stone Photo Library/London for page 45 (right); John Topham Picture Library for
page 30 (top right); Zefa Picture Library (UK) Limited for pages 11 (bottom), 16, 26
and 37.

Cover photograph by Rex Features Limited.

Illustrations by Clifford Meadway pages 2, 3, 31; David Mostyn pages 24, 25, 46, 47;
David Parkins page 34.